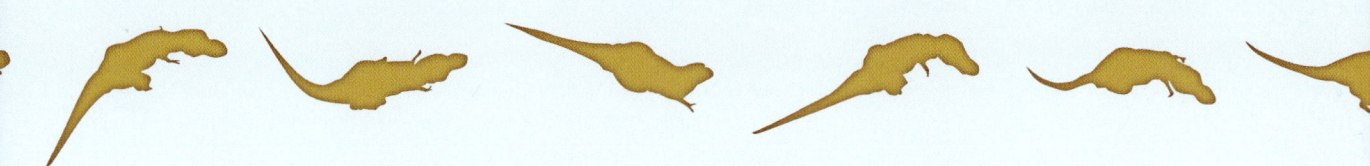

The Age of Dinosaurs

Meet Scipionyx

Written by Sheryn Knight
Illustrations by Leonello Calvetti and Luca Massini

New York

Published in 2015 by Cavendish Square Publishing, LLC
243 5th Avenue, Suite 136, New York, NY 10016

Copyright © 2015 by Cavendish Square Publishing, LLC

First Edition

No part of this publication may be reproduced, stored in a retrieval system, or transmitted in any form or by any means—electronic, mechanical, photocopying, recording, or otherwise—without the prior permission of the copyright owner. Request for permission should be addressed to Permissions, Cavendish Square Publishing, 243 5th Avenue, Suite 136, New York, NY 10016. Tel (877) 980-4450; fax (877) 980-4454.

Website: cavendishsq.com

This publication represents the opinions and views of the author based on his or her personal experience, knowledge, and research. The information in this book serves as a general guide only. The author and publisher have used their best efforts in preparing this book and disclaim liability rising directly or indirectly from the use and application of this book.

CPSIA Compliance Information: Batch #WS14CSQ

All websites were available and accurate when this book was sent to press.

Library of Congress Cataloging-in-Publication Data

Knight, Sheryn, 1967- author.
Meet Scipionyx / Sheryn Knight.
pages cm. — (The age of dinosaurs)
Includes index.
ISBN 978-1-62712-791-2 (hardcover) ISBN 978-1-62712-792-9 (paperback) ISBN 978-1-62712-793-6 (ebook)
1. Scipionyx—Juvenile literature. 2. Dinosaurs—Juvenile literature. I. Title.

QE862.S3K625 2015
567.912—dc23

2014006640

Editorial Director: Dean Miller
Copy Editor: Cynthia Roby
Art Director: Jeffrey Talbot
Designer: Douglas Brooks
Photo Researcher: J8 Media
Production Manager: Jennifer Ryder-Talbot
Production Editor: David McNamara
Illustrations by Leonello Calvetti and Luca Massini

The photographs in this book are used by permission and through the courtesy of: lorenzobovi/Shutterstock.com, 8; Ghedoghedo/File:Scipionyx samniticus 232.jpg/Wikimedia Commons, 20; G.dallorto/File:9122 - Milano, Museo storia naturale - Scipionyx samniticus - Foto Giovanni Dall'Orto 22-Apr-2007a.jpg/Wikimedia Commons, 21.

Printed in the United States of America

CONTENTS

1	A CHANGING WORLD	4
2	A DIMINUTIVE DINOSAUR	6
3	FINDING SCIPIONYX	8
4	BIRTH	10
5	SEARCHING FOR FOOD	13
6	AFTER THE STORM	15
7	DANGER ON THE SHORE	17
8	INSIDE SCIPIONYX	18
9	UNEARTHING SCIPIONYX	20
10	THE SAURICHIAN FAMILY	22
11	THE GREAT EXTINCTION	24
12	A DINOSAUR'S FAMILY TREE	26
	A SHORT VOCABULARY OF DINOSAURS	28
	DINOSAUR WEBSITES	30
	MUSEUMS	31
	INDEX	32

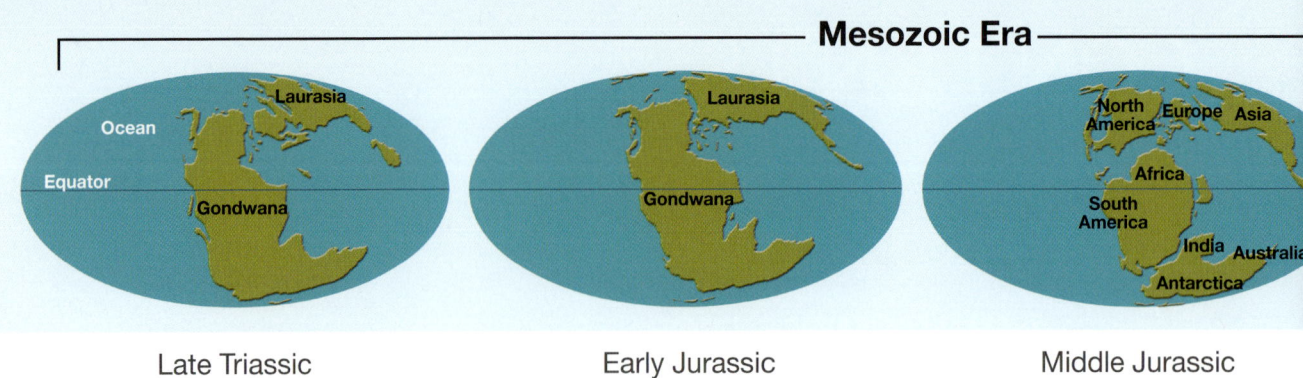

Mesozoic Era

Late Triassic
227 – 206 million years ago.

Early Jurassic
206 – 176 million years ago.

Middle Jurassic
176 – 159 million years ago.

A CHANGING WORLD

Earth's long history began 4.6 billion years ago. Dinosaurs were among the most fascinating life forms from Earth's long past.

The word "dinosaur" originates from the Greek words *deinos* and *sauros*, which together mean "fearfully great lizards."

To understand dinosaurs we need to understand geological time, the lifetime of our planet. Earth's history is divided into eras, periods, epochs, and ages. The dinosaur era, called the Mesozoic era, is divided in three periods: Triassic, which lasted 42 million years; Jurassic, 61 million years; and Cretaceous, 79 million years. Dinosaurs ruled the world for 160 million years.

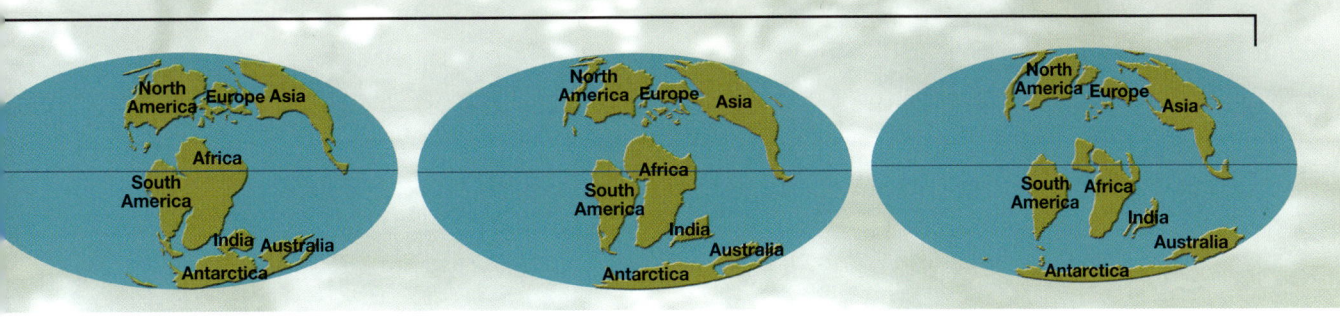

Late Jurassic
159 – 144 million years ago.

Early Cretaceous
144 – 99 million years ago.

Late Cretaceous
99 – 65 million years ago.

Man and dinosaurs never met. This is because dinosaurs had become extinct nearly 65 million years before man's appearance on Earth.

The dinosaur world differed from our world. The climate was warmer, the continents were different, and grass did not even exist!

A DIMINUTIVE DINOSAUR

Scipionyx, pronounced sip-ee-ON-ix, is a Saurischian, or "lizard-hipped," dinosaur of the suborder *Theropoda*. An ancestor of the bird, Scipionyx was a carnivore, or meat-eating dinosaur. It was also bipedal, meaning that the dinosaur moved about on its hind limbs alone. Scipionyx, which means "Scipio's claw," is a genus of *compsognathid theropod* dinosaur. It roamed Earth around 113 million years ago during the Early Cretaceous period in what is now Italy. The dinosaur was named after Scipione Breislak, an eighteenth-century geologist.

Little is known about Scipionyx, especially because to date only one fossil has been discovered. The fossil was that of a very young Scipionyx that paleontologists nicknamed "Skippy." This fossil measures about 18–20 inches (45–50 centimeters) long, and less than 5 inches (12 cm) in height. Its head, measuring just over

2 inches (5 cm) long, has enormous eye sockets and a short muzzle. The jaws hold about fifty sharp teeth. Two in the upper jaw were longer than the others and were used to hold onto its prey. Paleontologists estimate the young dinosaur's body to have weighed about 1 pound (500 grams).

Because of this fossil's tiny size, paleontologists believe that the adult Scipionyx was a rather small dinosaur. It probably measured about 6.5 feet (2 meters) in length and 3.3 feet (1 m) in height. It is estimated to have weighed around 130 pounds (59 kilograms).

FINDING SCIPIONYX

Scipionyx roamed Earth during the Cretaceous period about 113 million years ago. Its home was an island located in the middle of the Tethys Ocean, between Africa and Eurasia—the geographical name that describes the combined large area of land that was Europe and Asia. Earth's continents, however, have since changed. Today, the area is known as the southern region of Italy, and all that is left of the Tethys Ocean is the Mediterranean Sea.

Italy

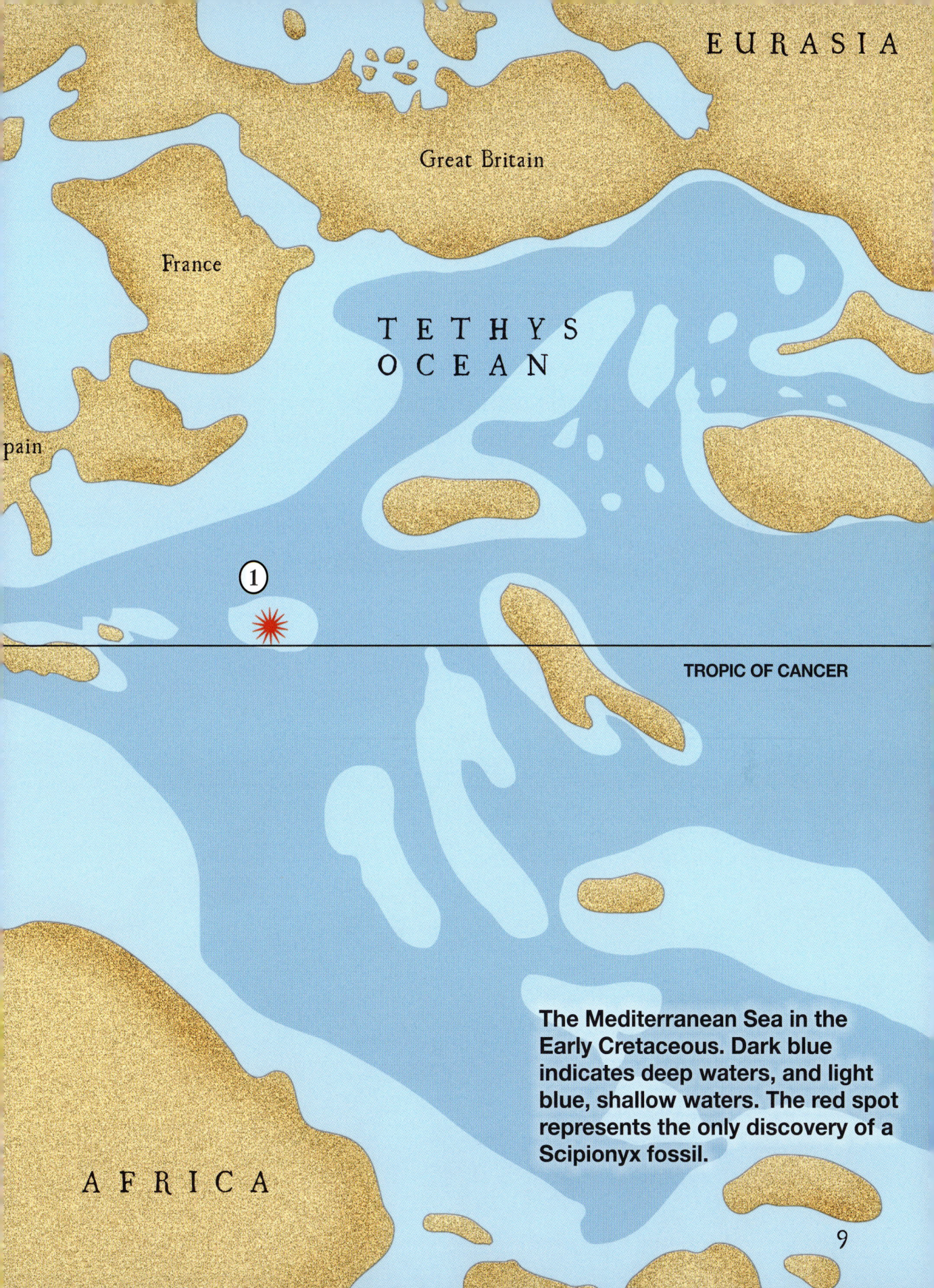

The Mediterranean Sea in the Early Cretaceous. Dark blue indicates deep waters, and light blue, shallow waters. The red spot represents the only discovery of a Scipionyx fossil.

BIRTH

The female Scipionyx built her nest in a sheltered and sandy place along the coast of the dinosaur's flat, tropical island home. She laid her clutch—or nest of eggs—among the plant life and low bushes.

There were only a few predators on the island that could endanger the babies, or hatchlings. But the young Scipionyx was very self-sufficient. This meant that the dinosaur did not have to stay in the nest, was able to walk, and did not have to depend on its mother for food. Still, the mother watched over the nesting area.

SEARCHING FOR FOOD

Paleontologists believe that Scipionyx darted along the ground chasing and eating flying insects. Because of their characteristics, scientists have concluded that Scipionyx were also predators. The dinosaurs had long, light-built skulls with jaws of sharp teeth. With strong, powerful legs and stiff tails used for balance, Scipionyx were likely swift and agile hunters. Their diet included a variety of fish that had washed ashore, smaller lizards, and other small vertebrates, or animals with backbones.

AFTER THE STORM

Tropical storms struck seasonally on the island where Scipionyx lived. The brutal winds would often wash large amounts of fish and shrimp onto the sandy shores. Lagoon waters became too salty and stagnant—meaning that they did not flow. The waters then became toxic and depleted of oxygen. The marine life—or the animals that lived in the waters—were then unable to breathe. Stranded on the shores, they then became prey for Scipionyx.

DANGER ON THE SHORE

Tidal flats are wetlands that are created when mud is washed ashore. They are also called mudflats. Younger Scipionyx would sometimes wander out onto the muddy surface in search of food. They had to be careful because scavengers and larger predators, such as crocodiles, would wait for Scipionyx. The sticky mud caused the dinosaurs to slow down and sometimes they became stuck. Predators then would find it easy to capture the young dinosaurs.

INSIDE SCIPIONYX

Scipionyx walked on its hind legs, had a long tail, and small forearms. Its head, mouth, and teeth were quite large. The dinosaur had a two-part abdominal cavity. Its lungs and heart were in one section, and the liver and guts in the other. A small wishbone, like that of birds, is found in the dinosaur's chest area. Some paleontologists believe that the dinosaur's body may have been covered with primitive feathers. No feathers, however, were found in its fossil.

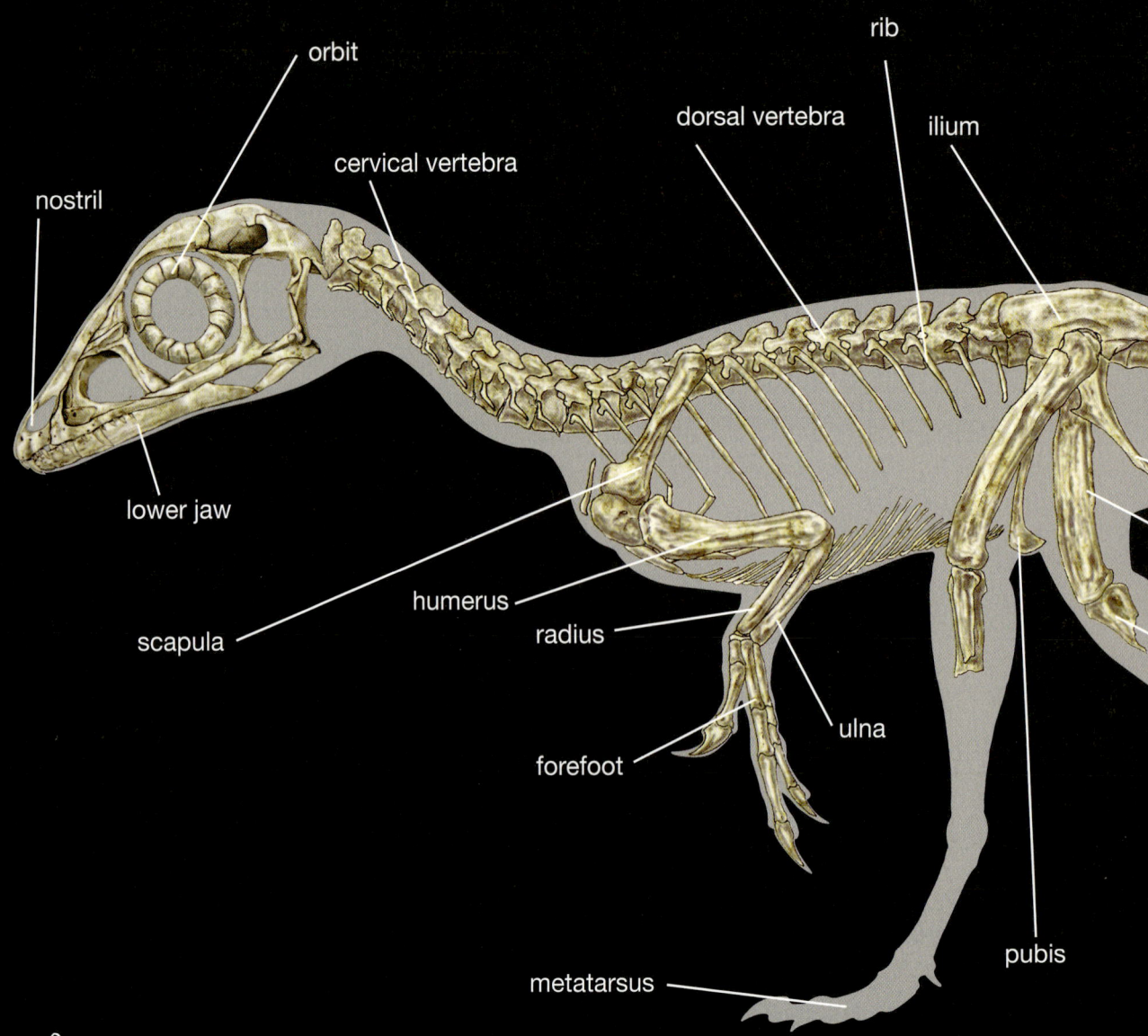

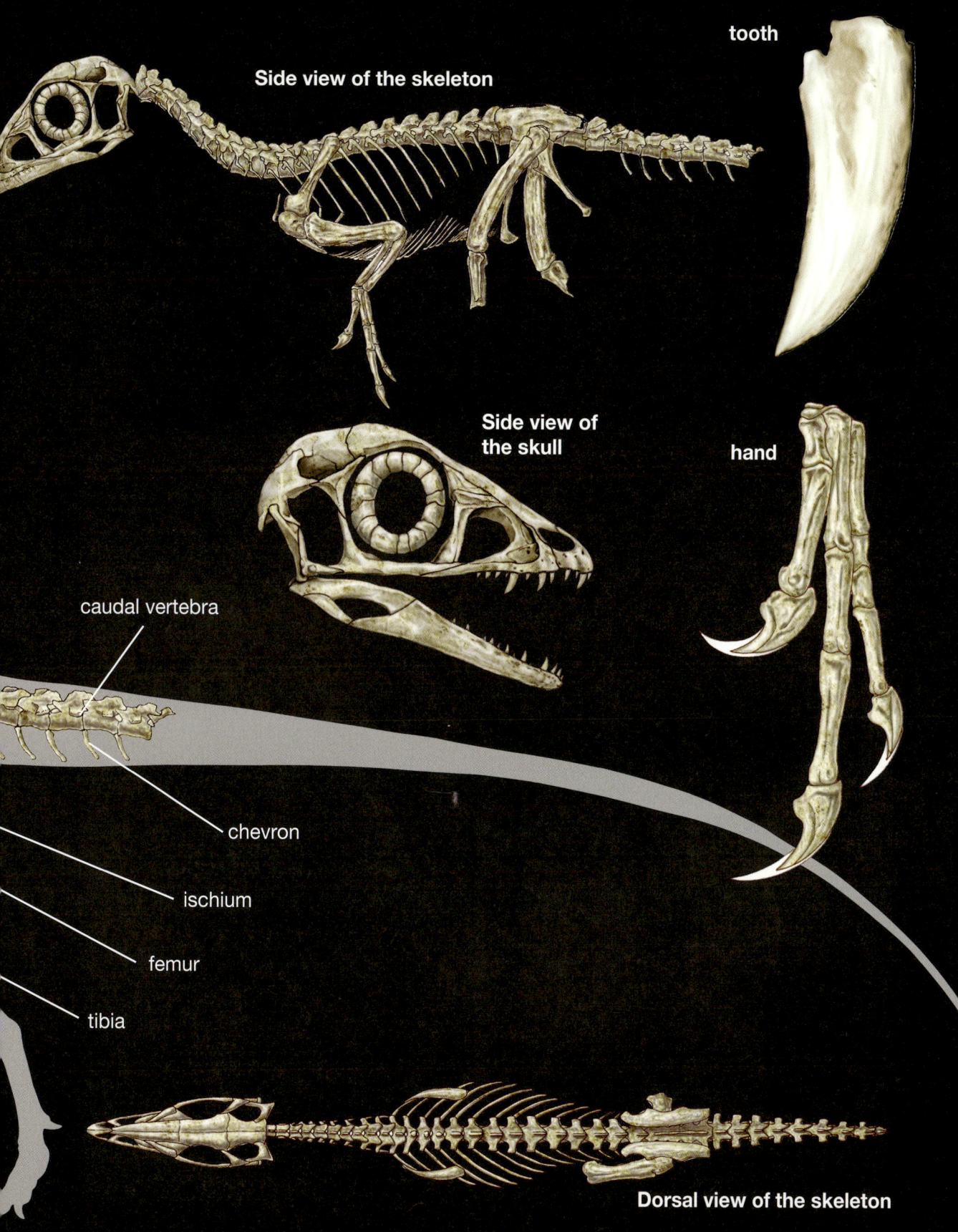

UNEARTHING SCIPIONYX

The only Scipionyx fossil found to date is that of a baby. Paleontologists believe that the young dinosaur was about three days old. It was unearthed in 1981 in the Pietraroja limestone formation near Pietraroja, Italy, about 50 miles (80 kilometers) north of Naples. It measures 20 inches (0.5 m) long and is 110 million years old. The discovery was made by amateur paleontologist Giovanni Todesco, who at first thought that he had unearthed a type of bird. In 1992, Scipionyx was identified as the first Italian dinosaur.

A fossil of Scipionyx, featuring its long neck and birdlike skull.

A close-up of the feet on the first Scipionyx fossil ever discovered.

THE SAURICHIAN FAMILY

Discovery sites of the "lizard-hipped" dinosaurs are shown on these pages.

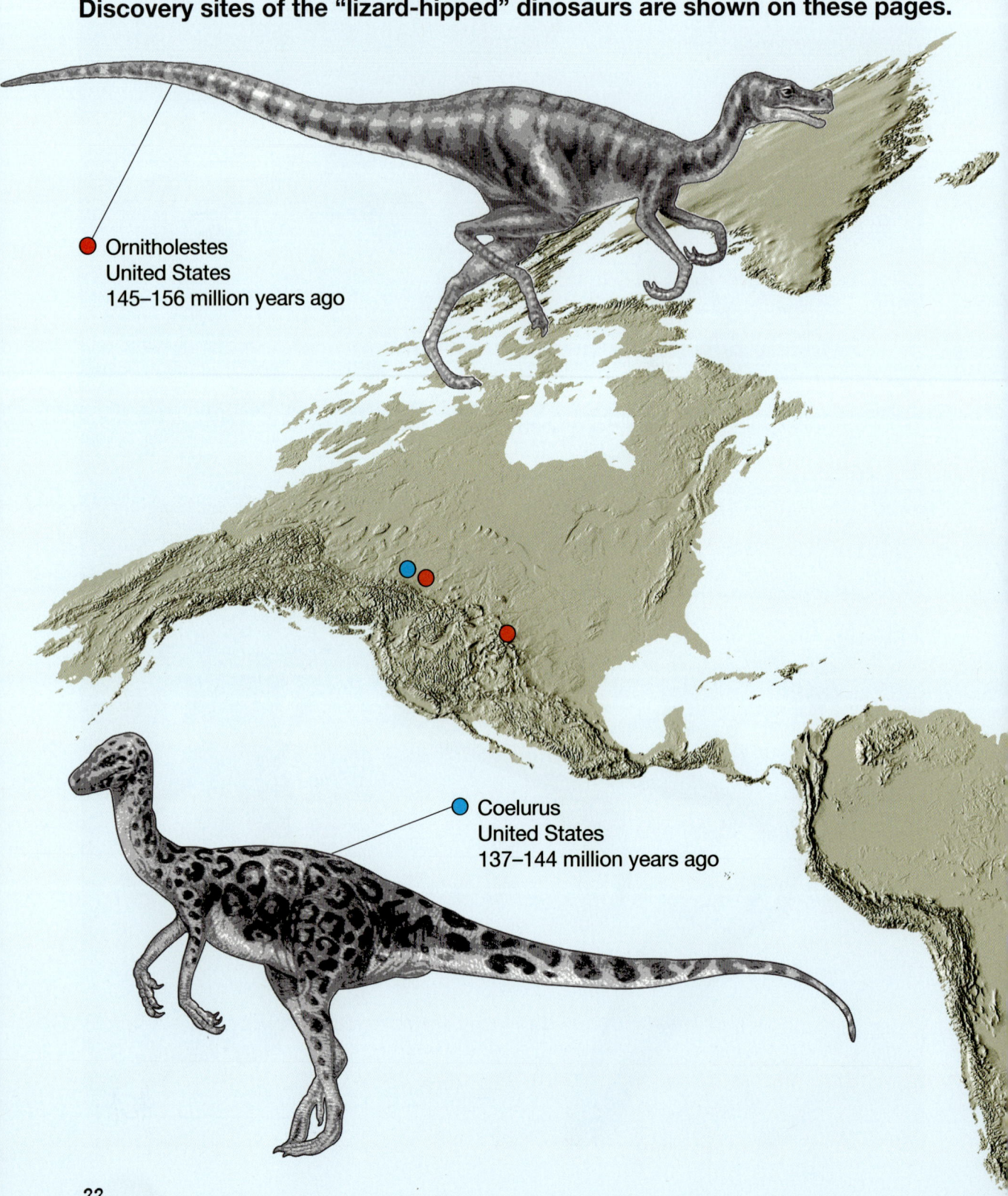

- Ornitholestes
  United States
  145–156 million years ago

- Coelurus
  United States
  137–144 million years ago

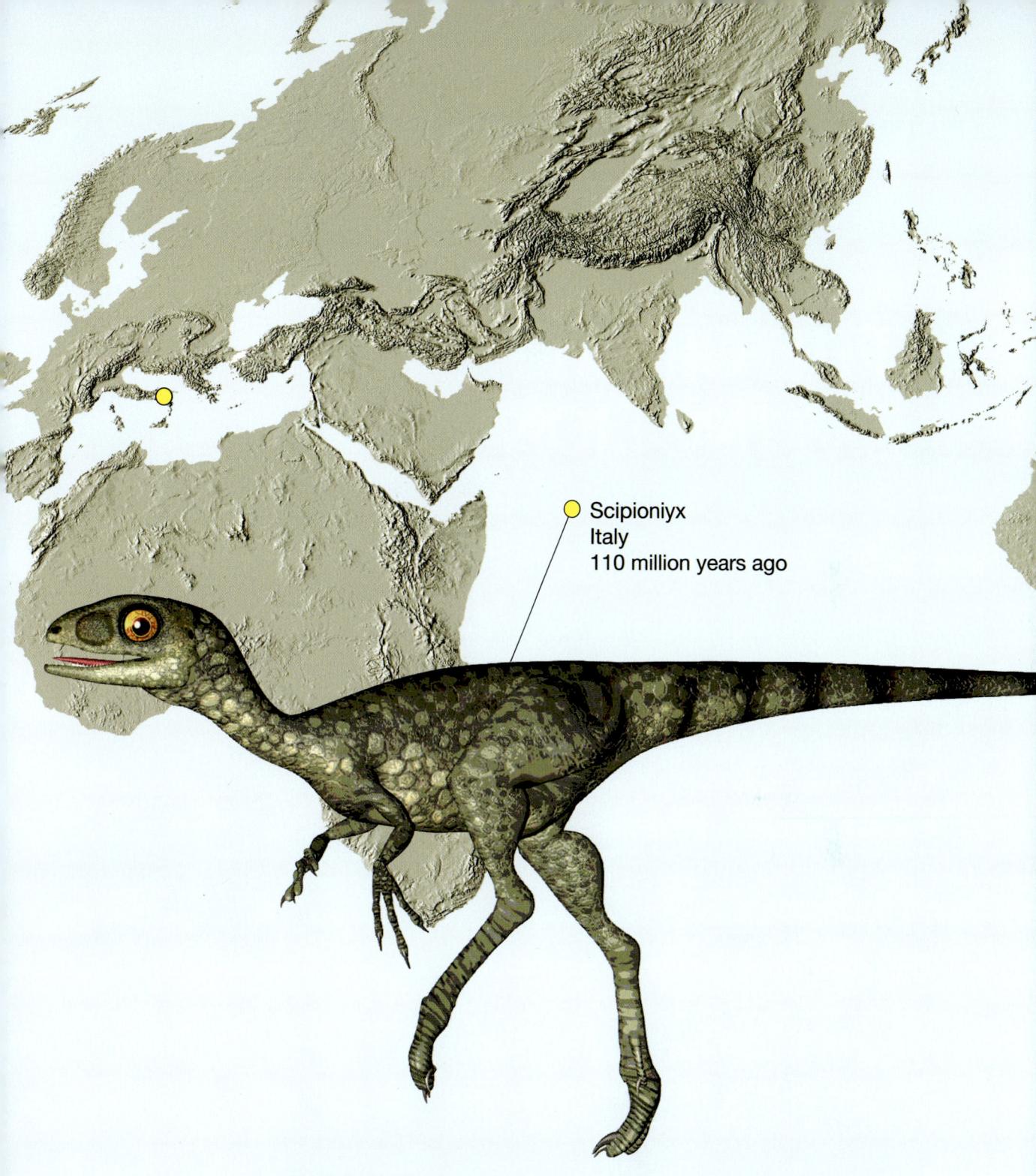

Scipioniyx
Italy
110 million years ago

The Saurischian dinosaurs (order *Saurischia*) were the ancestors of birds. They are divided into two groups: the *sauropodomorpha*, or four-legged herbivores, and the *theropods*, or two-legged carnivores. The oldest-known dinosaurs, Eoraptor and Herrerasaurus, are Saurischians.

THE GREAT EXTINCTION

Scientists believe a large meteorite hit the Earth, causing the extinction of the dinosaurs. A wide crater caused by a meteorite exactly 65 million years ago has been located along the coast of Mexico. The dust suspended in the air by the impact would have obscured the sunlight for a long time, causing a drastic drop in temperature and killing many plants.

The plant-eating dinosaurs would have starved or frozen to death. Meat-eating dinosaurs would have also died without their food supply. However, some scientists believe dinosaurs did not die out completely and that present-day chickens and other birds are, in a way, the descendants of the large dinosaurs.

A DINOSAUR'S FAMILY TREE

The oldest dinosaur fossils are 220–225 million years old and have been found all over the world.

Dinosaurs are divided into two groups. Saurischians are similar to reptiles, with the pubic bone directed forward, while the Ornithischians are like birds, with the pubic bone directed backward.

Saurischians are subdivided in two main groups: Sauropodomorphs, to which quadrupeds and vegetarians belong; and Theropods, which include bipeds and predators.

Ornithischians are subdivided into three large groups: Thyreophorans, which include the quadrupeds Stegosaurians and Ankylosaurians; Ornithopods; and Marginocephalians, which are subdivided into the bipedal Pachycephalosaurians and the mainly quadrupedal Ceratopsians.

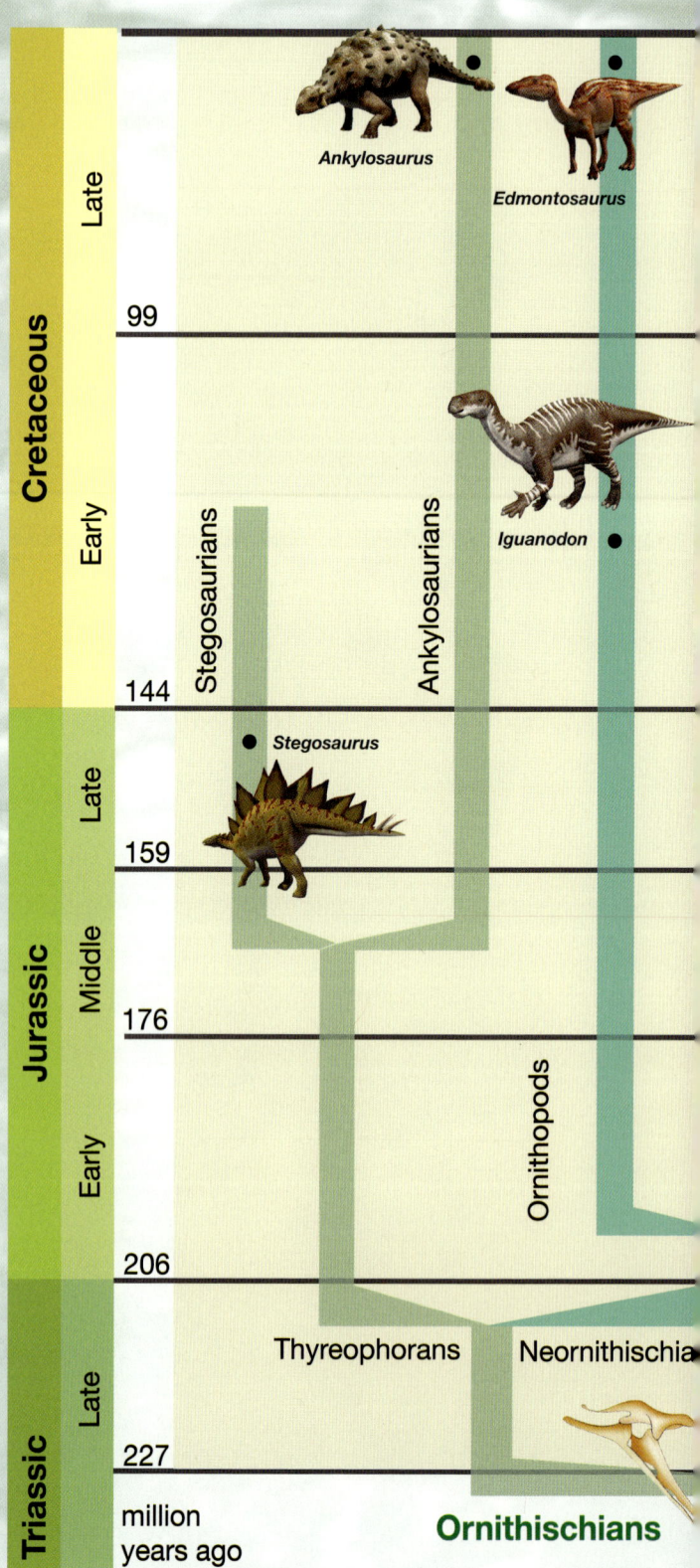

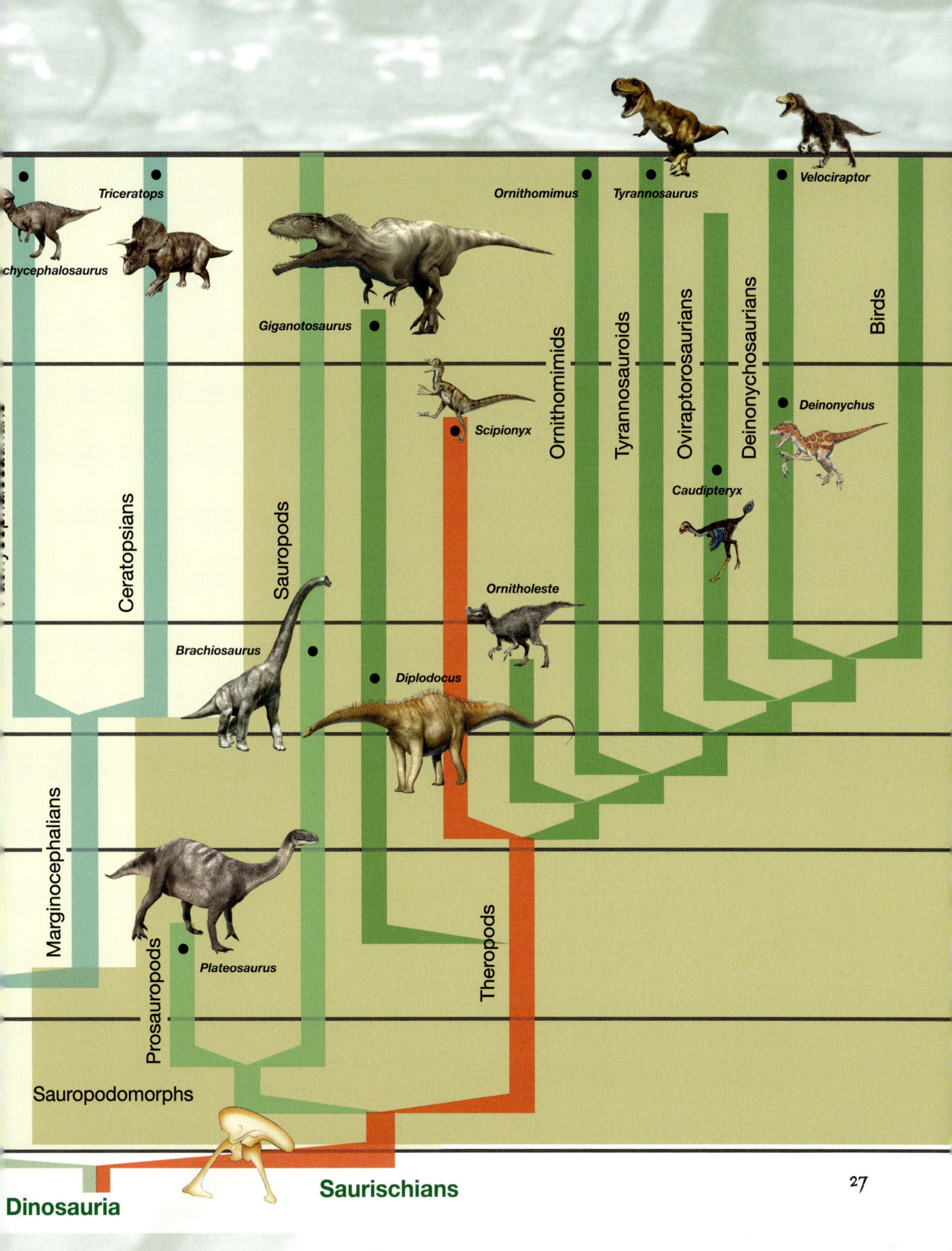

A SHORT VOCABULARY OF DINOSAURS

Bipedal: pertaining to an animal moving on two feet alone, almost always those of the hind legs.

Bone: hard tissue made mainly of calcium phosphate; single element of the skeleton.

Carnivore: a meat-eating animal.

Caudal: pertaining to the tail.

Cenozoic Era (Caenozoic, Tertiary Era): the interval of geological time between 65 million years ago and present day.

Cervical: pertaining to the neck.

Claws: the fingers and toes of predator animals end with pointed and sharp nails, called claws. Those of plant-eaters end with blunt nails, called hooves.

Cretaceous Period: the interval of geological time between 144 and 65 million years ago.

Egg: a large cell enclosed in a porous shell produced by reptiles and birds to reproduce themselves.

Epoch: a memorable date or event.

Evolution: changes in the character states of organisms, species, and higher ranks through time.

Extinct: when something, such as a species of animal, is no longer existing.

Feathers: outgrowth of the skin of birds and some dinosaurs, used in flight and in providing insulation and protection for the body. They evolved from reptilian scales.

Forage: to wander in search of food.

Fossil: evidence of life in the past. Not only bones, but footprints and trails made by animals, as well as dung, eggs or plant resin, when fossilized, are fossils.

Herbivore: a plant-eating animal.

Jurassic Period: the interval of geological time between 206 and 144 million years ago.

Mesozoic Era (Mesozoic, Secondary Era): the interval of geological time between 248 and 65 million years ago.

Pack: a group of predator animals acting together to capture their prey.

Paleontologist: a scientist who studies and reconstructs the prehistoric life.

Paleozoic Era (Paleozoic, Primary Era): the interval of geological time between 570 and 248 million years ago.

Predator: an animal that preys on other animals for food.

Raptor (raptorial): a bird of prey, such as an eagle, hawk, falcon, or owl.

Rectrix (plural rectrices): any of the larger feathers in a bird's tail that are important in helping its flight direction.

Scavenger: an animal that eats dead animals.

Skeleton: a structure of an animal's body made of several different bones. One primary function is to protect delicate organs such as the brain, lungs, and heart.

Skin: the external, thin layer of the animal body. Skin cannot fossilize, unless it is covered by scales, feathers, or fur.

Skull: bones that protect the brain and the face.

Teeth: tough structures in the jaws used to hold, cut, and sometimes process food.

Terrestrial: living on land.

Triassic Period: the interval of geological time between 248 and 206 million years ago.

Unearth: to find something that was buried beneath the earth.

Vertebrae: the single bones of the backbone; they protect the spinal cord.

DINOSAUR WEBSITES

Dino Database
www.dinodatabase.com
Get the latest news on dinosaur research and discoveries. This site is pretty advanced, so you may need help from a teacher or parent to find what you're looking for.

Dinosaurs for Kids
www.kidsdinos.com
There's basic information about most dinosaur types, and you can play dinosaur games, vote for your favorite dinosaur, and learn about the study of dinosaurs, paleontology.

Dinosaur Train
pbskids.org/dinosaurtrain
From the PBS show *Dinosaur Train*, you can watch videos, print out pages to color, play games, and learn lots of facts about so many dinosaurs!

Discovery Channel Dinosaur Videos
discovery.com/video-topics/other/other-topics-dinosaur-videos.htm
Watch almost 100 videos about the life of dinosaurs!

The Natural History Museum
www.nhm.ac.uk/kids-only/dinosaurs
Take a quiz to see how much you know about dinosaurs—or a quiz to tell you what type of dinosaur you'd be! There's also a fun directory of dinosaurs, including some cool 3-D views of your favorites.

MUSEUMS

American Museum of Natural History, New York, NY
www.amnh.org

Carnegie Museum of Natural History, Pittsburgh, PA
www.carnegiemnh.org

Denver Museum of Nature and Science, Denver, CO
www.dmns.org

Dinosaur National Monument, Dinosaur, CO
www.nps.gov/dino

The Field Museum, Chicago, IL
fieldmuseum.org

University of California Museum of Paleontology, Berkeley, CA
www.ucmp.berkeley.edu

Museum of the Rockies, Bozeman, MT
www.museumoftherockies.org

National Museum of Natural History, Smithsonian Institution,
Washington, DC
www.mnh.si.edu

Royal Tyrrell Museum of Palaeontology, Drumheller, Canada
www.tyrrellmuseum.com

Sam Noble Museum of Natural History, Norman, OK
www.snomnh.ou.edu

Yale Peabody Museum of Natural History, New Haven, CT
peabody.yale.edu

INDEX

Page numbers in **boldface** are illustrations.

Breislak, Scipione, 6

carnivore, 6, **23**
clutch, 10
Cretaceous period, 4, **5**, 6, 8, **9**, **26–27**

epoch, 4

food, 13, 15, 17
fossil, 6, 7, **9**, 18, 20, **21**, 26

Jurassic period, **4–5**, **26–27**

Mesozoic era, **4–5**
mudflats, 17

paleontologist, 6, 7, 13, 18, 20

Scipionyx
  size, 6–7
  where discovered, 8, **9**, 20, **22–23**
  young, 10
skeleton, 7, **18–19**
"Skippy", 6
skull, 13, **19**

teeth, 6, 13, 18
Todesco, Giovanni, 20
Triassic period, **4**, **26–27**